Charles,

The Best Bu

on the Planet

Tell Your Story!!
Your Story Matters!!!

B

The Best Business Card

on the Planet

The Ultimate Strategy
for Dominating a Market
and Getting More People
to Discover You, Hire You, and Refer You

Bob Regnerus
Game Changers Multimedia

Published by Game Changers Multimedia (Bob Regnerus)
PO Box 251, Palos Heights, IL 60463
Phone: 1–877–349–2615

Printed in the United States of America
Editing and design by www.CompassRose.com

ISBN-13: 978-0-9858875-2-0
ISBN-10: 0985887524

This book is dedicated to all the professionals, consultants, coaches, and business leaders who want to do more and be more.

The book is for those passionate people with a mission and message that the world needs to know. May this book inspire you to achieve your goal of getting that message heard.

To my wife Arlene, my daughters Bethany and Anna, and to all my friends and colleagues who have been part of my journey over the years in the world of being an entrepreneur.

Special thanks to my editor Joanne Asala of Compass Rose Horizons for her help putting this book together. Joanne can be found online at www.compassrose.com.

About the Author

 **Bob Regnerus** is a die-hard Chicago White Sox fan who didn't pursue a baseball career after high school despite his good arm and glove. Much to his dismay, Bob was never able to consistently put the bat on the ball. So with Major League Baseball off the table, he pursued a career in business and soon realized he enjoyed being the boss more than being bossed around!

Since 1995 Bob has been running his own companies, and he has finally learned how to hit home runs – not with a bat, but through developing his skills in direct marketing and building platforms for his clients.

Bob is a coach, author, speaker, and book producer. His unique abilities are in helping you build a platform, crafting your unique story, and getting the word out about your business so you become the go-to expert in your market. His platforms have always been designed to produce home runs for his clients by attracting high-quality leads to a client's high-fee products and services.

Bob has worked with many prestigious institutions, including the Dartmouth School of Business and Miracle-Ear®, as well as with hundreds of CEOs, authors, business leaders, athletes, coaches, professionals, and business owners.

Bob is the author of a self-published book titled *Big Ticket eCommerce* as well as *The Official Get Rich Guide to Information Marketing on the Internet,* published by Entrepreneur Press. He is also a contributing author to three other books.

Bob co-hosts a radio show on AM560-WIND in Chicago called "The Game Changers Radio Show," where he interviews business leaders and entrepreneurs each week.

Learn more at www.GameChangersRadioShow.com

For any questions about publishing *your* book, please see www.MyBookDone.com and watch the FREE webinar *Self-Publish!*

You can contact Bob Regnerus at Bob@RJRComputing.com or (877) 349–2615.

Learn more about Bob at www.BobRegnerus.com

Foreword

If you are a passionate leader and desire to broadcast your mission and message to the world, then this book is for you. To get through the clutter, noise, and overwhelm of your audience, you need a strategy to get your message heard.

I believe there's an ultimate strategy to get this done, one that has existed for thousands of years. Knowing this strategy and implementing it will be the key to building your platform and getting more people to discover you, hire you, and refer you.

How many of these words accurately describe what you are looking for?

- Attention
- Influence
- Celebrity
- Authority
- Significance
- Credibility
- Integrity
- Opportunity
- Achievement
- Leverage
- Advantage

The longer I live, the more I am convinced that people just want to be heard. More than a craving for food, sleep, or money, people have a deep, embedded need for someone to acknowledge they exist.

A strange phenomenon occurs today. I'd call it a complex paradox of sorts. Would you agree with me that at the very same time we have amazing tools and resources to broadcast a message to billions of people with ease, the amount of noise and people clamoring to be heard actually makes it nearly impossible for people to hear you?

The advent of social media and smartphones gives every single person who possesses these assets an efficient and powerful platform to voice their opinion, offer knowledge, and gather a following.

By virtue of you reading this book, I am safe to assume you have a message or mission that you want to broadcast, and you are asking yourself one of two questions:

1) Why have very few people responded to my message in the past and what can I do to fix it?

2) What is the best way for this message inside of me to be heard and make the most impact?

Consider your strengths as an entrepreneur. Do any of these statements apply to you?

INTRODUCTION

The Convenient Truths
of Today's Business World

As a leader, you know that implementing your desire and need to broadcast your mission and message is difficult, but not impossible. To play this game, you must understand the rules and the playing field you have chosen to step on to.

Business is a great and challenging exercise for anyone. Success does not come easily, although you'd think so by watching TV and the movies. I've read enough biographies of successful men and women to know that very few have it dropped in their laps. Most success stories begin with challenges, failures, and suffering. But this is the game we've chosen, so let's examine the truths of the business world.

Truth #1 – People Don't Trust You

Trust is a fleeting character trait these days. I personally have been burned by so many so-called "trustworthy" people that there are calluses over my scabs of healed-over wounds.

How many of us feel like the great cartoon character we all love, Charlie Brown? We all have sprinted towards Lucy in our own way and whiffed mightily as she pulled that football back and watched us propel ourselves in the air and fall squarely on our asses.

Point is, we've all been burned. Multiple times.

We're conditioned by our experiences not to trust people. We're let down by friends, colleagues, politicians, religious leaders, teachers, salesmen, and even our loved ones. It's often at the time of us fully believing in another person that we are dealt the harsh blow of reality, and once again our trust is taken advantage of.

This, my friends, is the reality of the world we live in. If you just imagine the amount of distrust people have in their own relationships, you can also assume they have even less trust when it comes to business relationships.

Who trusts a salesman to not screw them over on a deal? Who doesn't think their lawyer, doctor, or accountant is charging way more than they are worth? Who hasn't paid a dollar for something to later find it was readily available for fifty cents?

Trust is a RARE commodity these days, and becoming a person who is considered "trustworthy" is an uphill battle in the most accurate sense of the word.

We have a general lack of trust towards most businesses today, and when we find that rare business we do trust, we protect that connection as best we can to avoid the perilous search of finding someone new we can trust.

Our goal as business people is to be that person people

can trust because once we cut through the skepticism and defense systems, we can have an amazing business with customers and clients who truly love and trust us as their source.

Truth #2 – People Are Overwhelmed

Rare is the person in our life with loads of free time, a general lack of concern for the immediate, and the carefree attitude of a California surfer.

What I mean to say is that people have too much to do and very little time to do it in.

The average American is working fifty-plus hours a week, commuting ten hours a week, sleeping about six hours a night, eating dinner in about thirteen minutes, and spending the rest of the time trying to make it to all their kids' baseball games and school concerts without going crazy.

Then, to make matters worse, we attach a smartphone to our hip that connects us 24x7 to e-mail, text messages, Facebook, Twitter, and funny videos of cats. The good news is we're spending less time watching TV even though we have 6,793 channels to flip through.

Try this sometime. Ask any one of your friends at any time one of these questions:

- "How are things at work?"

- "How are things at home?"
- "What does your schedule look like next week?"

The answers you'll get 93% of the time are "Busy!" "Busy!!" and "Busy!!!"

Our minds have little time to stop and be quiet – in fact, we're quite jumpy when things are quiet on the rare occasion. We simply are conditioned as a society to be busy, to desire to be busy, and to pretend as if we're busy (even when we're not). We're addicted to noise as a result; we are quite capable and proficient at shutting out ANYTHING that will cause us to go over the edge.

Overwhelm is the standard operating procedure of most of Western society. So we are not surprised that media and the advertisers do all they can to find new and innovative ways to interrupt our day, invade our media, and scream loudly for our attention. They have to do this in order to survive! Perhaps you've had to do the same?

Overwhelmed, anxious people make difficult prospects, unless you're selling them liquor or Xanax. (I'm kidding . . . actually I'm not.)

We have to offer our potential customers a means to learn more about us as well as our products and services in a way that doesn't increase their state of overwhelm. Ideally, we connect with them and reduce that anxious state so that they clearly see us as a great solution for them.

Truth #3 – People Don't Buy Stuff, They Buy You

I've consulted with many business owners over the years who have made a strategic error when it comes to marketing. They've managed to reduce their value to the products and services they offer, and feel that the only way to make more sales and grow a company is to offer more products, more services, and win a client's heart by logically stating a laundry list of benefits.

They purposefully remove themselves from the equation and hope they can win a client's heart by merely making an argument based on a list of facts. For any professional service provider reading this, please hear me loud and clear.

There are DOZENS if not HUNDREDS of professionals your prospects can hire to solve their problem. Most of them can boast a similar if not larger list of "stuff" that is meant to impress the client. What you do and what you offer is simply not enough of an argument for a client to hire you unless you truly are the only option available. However, most of you are faced with the reality of competing with multiple service providers that offer similar, if not superior products and services to a market.

But there's a secret they don't know, and if you examine your own behavior you'd see it, too – there is no one on the planet who is the same as you! You, by virtue of your skill set, story, personality, and characteristics, are unique. Your uniqueness is your advantage, and if you can artfully and eloquently communicate your uniqueness in your marketing, you will discover that people will desire to do business with you FIRST because of who you are, and SECONDLY by what you do.

Just look at your own behavior as a consumer and think logically about this. If you were looking for a financial planner, would you care that one has twenty investment vehicles and one has two thousand, or would you be more interested in their ability to understand and exhibit a track record working for someone in your situation? Would you rather have your children see a dentist who demonstrates her desire and passion for young people's teeth and giving them a good experience at her office, or simply choose the closest one that takes your insurance?

No matter if you are a solo professional or the head of a large organization, please understand that people do business with people, and the more you can be a person with your prospects, the better chance they will become your long-term clients.

Truth #4 – Stories Sell

Knowing that people are going to invest in you because of *you*, it becomes imperative that you learn the art of storytelling and conversation.

It's simply not enough to state implicitly who you are and list your credentials and work experience. That's what a resume is for. You have to capture the mind and heart of your potential customer by telling a story.

Stories are what connect people to each other, and if you pay attention, you see that even the largest companies are using this message in their advertising.

I'm seeing large companies embracing this concept. I'm thinking now about some of the Ford Motor Company commercials that feature people test driving a Ford and comparing it to their Chevy. I'm thinking about the various travel bureaus that have created great story-based advertising to entice travelers to their state – Michigan, Colorado, California, and Florida stand out in my memory.

Gifted copywriters are paid millions of dollars to craft and create stories that connect products and services to customers.

But you don't have to be a highly paid copywriter to tell your story. You just need the confidence and guts to do it. Believe it or not, many people are afraid to tell their story because of a worry over privacy, embarrassment, or lack of understanding. Telling your story might be the very best marketing decision you ever make.

Dave Thomas sold a lot of hamburgers telling his story. Lee Iacocca sold a lot of Chryslers telling his story. Steve Jobs sold a lot of electronics by sharing his passions with the world. If it works for Fortune 100 companies, it will work even better for you.

Truth #5 – Tricks and Gimmicks Don't Last Long

For a short time, every business has the ability to use smoke and mirrors and crafty wordsmithing to sell a few widgets. It's great to get customers to your door and get some cash, but is it creating a long-term asset for you?

I recall the furor here in the Midwest several years back over Krispy Kreme donuts. Now, I'm not denying it was a rush getting a box of warm, glazed donuts fresh from the line, but once people recovered from the sugar high, they realized it's just not sensible to eat these soft, gooey, sugar-covered, deep-fried, heavenly donuts on a regular basis. (I have nothing against this company. Bravo to them for getting Wall Street and millions of people to fall in love with them. Quite an accomplishment in my opinion.)

How about the car dealership with the funny commercials, bouncy huts for the kids, and free hamburgers on the weekend? Once you get inside, if they aren't any different from every car dealer you've dealt with, you probably aren't buying, and you certainly aren't coming back.

What about the story of Domino's Pizza? They invented the idea of fresh, hot pizza delivered to your door in thirty minutes or less, but even the least-sophisticated palates soon discovered that tomato sauce, processed cheese, and cardboard crust didn't make a good pizza. Now you see Domino's working VERY hard to tell a story about the quality of their pizza and even admitting fully to their wrongs and faults. (This is a great case study for you.)

My advice is simple – if you have to gimmick your way to trick customers into giving you money, it's a dead-end business. Exit now before you get sued or go bankrupt. Find a business where people genuinely want what you have and appreciate you for providing it to them.

Truth #6 – The Free Line Has Moved to the Right

The Internet has opened the floodgates of information to the masses. Even though the public library has made information available to people for many years, the Internet, specifically Amazon.com and Google's ability to catalog information, has made information a commodity.

Not even a dozen years ago, some information was still difficult to obtain, and therefore was a resource people paid for. It's hard to imagine that any subject matter that matters to the masses is not already available at hundreds and thousands of websites for free, or contained within a book that costs less than $15.

Information still carries value, but only in one's ability to process it. This is a subject matter for a different book, but for this point, know that people have been conditioned to expect a great deal of valuable information to be made available to them at little or no charge. And by the way, your refusal to play ball according to these rules is not heroic, it's a death wish.

The quicker you realize that your market demands free information, the quicker you get to offering the real assets people *will* pay for – someone that can implement the knowledge for them or talk them through it.

You see, if you want to prove to someone you know how to manage money, you might as well go ahead and tell them how you manage money. If you don't, the CFP down the street will and will take a client away from you.

By telling people how *you* do something, you actually develop trust and credibility with them, and if your knowledge is sophisticated and complex, you can trust they will have no idea what to do with your knowledge other than hire you to execute it for them!

Truth #7 – People Prefer to Buy from Experts

An expert is someone who possesses the skill and desire to execute a certain task, solve a problem, or implement a solution. All things being equal, if someone has a problem and needs it solved, he or she will turn to an expert to either help get it done or do it entirely.

What we need to understand as professionals is that people prefer to do business with experts, especially when it comes to things that are extremely important to them, such as their health, wealth, family, career, education, home, transportation, and self-improvement.

Why would anyone care to help choose a college for their daughter by blindly choosing a planner from an ad and hiring them on the spot? Of course you're going to read the planner's website, download materials, look at references, read their book, watch their videos, find success stories, and schedule a visit. I'm sure it's the same for any professional.

Knowing that this is what people will likely do, it's your job as a professional to provide them the media and resources they can easily consume to discover your expertise.

People do business with experts, so what are you doing to establish yourself as one?

Is there a medium that does this better than others?

Section 1

Writing a Book

*The Ultimate Strategy for Getting More People
to Discover You, Hire You, and Refer You*

Book Authors Are Experts

You *need* to author a book. A book is the ultimate strategy for getting more people to discover you, hire you, and refer you because . . .

Book Authors Are Experts.

Obviously, there are levels of expertise, but you can't argue that authors have an advantage.

Scan your bookshelf right now if you are near it. Skip over the fictional books and focus in on the non-fiction business books you have there.

First of all, how many do you have, and secondly, look at the names on the spine. How do you feel about these authors? Are they experts? Probably so.

Quick, name a conference you have attended where none of the speakers authored a book.

Do you see where I'm going?

I don't think I need to stage a debate on the expertise of authors. I believe you know this and believe it like most people. Let's discuss instead some obvious advantages an author has over "commoners," keeping a focus on being an author who wants to target a group of customers or clients in a specific market over someone who does not.

Advantage #1: Only a Small Fraction of the World's Population Are Authors!

This goes without saying. If you decide to become an author and you go to a ballgame or concert, how many of the people in that crowd are published authors and would have a book on Amazon.com? Five, ten, twenty? Sitting in a crowd of 25,000 people, at a generous count of twenty authors, that's 0.0008 or .08% who are authors. That's a select club you are joining!

Advantage #2: Expert versus Salesman

Be open to what I'm about to say. If you are in business, you are always selling yourself.

We are talking about writing a business book; therefore, your goal in authoring a book is to sell yourself.

When talking about a book, we've got thousands of years of history on our side. Books are vehicles to deliver information. Perception is our friend. Books are not a threat to someone, and they do not scream, "I want to sell you something."

I want to encourage you to not abuse this privilege. When you author your book, be generous with great information and inspiration for your readers so that when they are done, they know more and are motivated to do more.

At the same time, do not miss the opportunity to let your readers know how you can serve them with the information you delivered them in your book.

There's a significant opportunity to teach, inspire, motivate, and sell in a vacuum. It's just you, one on one with your readers. By demonstrating your expertise, you can win over prospects and turn them into customers and clients. There will be very little resistance if you carefully build your case and give good information to the reader.

Advantage #3: Perception of Being a "Prescriber" versus a Salesman

Here's another take on perception. When you are considered an expert instead of a salesman, you have a different relationship with your reader.

Think for a moment. When you sit in the office of a doctor, and she prescribes medication, you go to the pharmacy and buy the meds. When a specialist orders tests and procedures, you get them done. Did you ever stop and think that the medical professional standing in front of you is *selling* to you? Probably not. They may not technically be selling to you, but they are telling you exactly how to spend your money (even if some of it is paid for by insurance). They are prescribing a solution.

My friends, this is the position you want: To be prescribing solutions to your reader instead of selling them. (Might I add that if you never write a book, you should still try to position yourself in such a way that your prospects consider you an expert and come to you for prescriptions!)

Advantage #4: You Can Charge Higher Fees

I don't need to pontificate on this. Experts get higher fees. Period. However, it's up to you to deliver the goods to justify the fees you charge. If you are just a pretender, it will catch up to you.

Advantage #5: Gain an Advantage over Your Competitor Who Doesn't Have a Book

There's nothing like creating leverage in a market. All things being equal, having a book creates huge advantages for you in a market. If there's any sort of decision-making process by your potential clients, you having a book is going to be a game changer, potentially swaying the opinions of your prospects.

Advantage #6: You Can Stop Chasing Business Because Clients Seek You

Something magical happens when you publish a book —

clients start to seek you out. This is the ultimate competitive advantage and positioning in a market.

When you can deploy your book into a market and get clients coming to you, it allows you to grow faster, decide which clients you want to work with, charge higher fees, and maintain leverage in the relationship. It's a great catalyst to foster new growth for an established business, and a great starter for a new venture.

Be forewarned – just writing a book will not cause a stampede to your door. You will need to deploy your marketing savvy and resources to get your book in the hands of prospects. But when you can tap into the demand of a market and offer them a tool like a book to help them fulfill that demand, that's a winner.

Advantage #7: All Your Clients and Prospects Are Better Educated About Your Biz

You may have never thought about this, but how much time do you spend in the sales process repeating yourself? Meaning, if you have three sales appointments in a day, do you find that you are repeating the same introductory information to those three prospects?

Think about how much time you spend dispensing information rather than discussing a prospect's needs and helping them make a purchase decision. If you could capture the basic "FAQs" of your business and educate your prospect, wouldn't it save you a lot of time delivering the pleasantries and introductory information?

Your book becomes a vehicle to educate your prospect about your business, about your products and services, about your systems, and about you. It does a great deal of heavy lifting for you and actually becomes an income-producing asset for your business.

Advantage #8: Speaking Opportunities on Stages of All Kinds

Authors get to speak in front of audiences – if they want.

One of the main reasons I chose to write my own book in 2007 was to get on stage because it was the best way I knew to get clients. For several years, I was on stages big and small, and every speaking engagement produced immediate income and client work.

We understand stages to mean physical platforms, but you also get invited to speak on virtual stages through webinars and teleseminars. These are highly effective ways to leverage your book and get new clients.

The key is that more stages open up to you when you have a book. Event promoters are reluctant to put anyone on stage. Their stage is a sacred platform, and they have a responsibility to the audience to produce a good event.

Authors provide promoters a safe pool of talent to find speakers because all they need to do is see you have a book, and perhaps skim it if they choose. Later, I'll outline the simple strategy on how to use your book to get speaking engagements.

I'd encourage every business owner to get comfortable with speaking in public, especially when you become an author. It creates tremendous leverage for your business when you can use your book to get speaking engagements that have your target clients in attendance.

**Advantage #9: Interviewers on Radio, TV,
and with Print Media NEED Content,
NEED Authors, and Welcome Your Pitch!**

Just like speaking on stages, you get the opportunity to be interviewed in the media when you have a book.

This is a tremendous way for you to gain credibility. Getting interviewed by a member of the traditional media further cements your authority. Interviews validate you and provide another platform for you to demonstrate your expertise. Each interview you do becomes an asset in your marketing down the road, especially if the media is archived for people to access in the future.

I host a radio show in Chicago on AM560-WIND (real radio!) called "The Game Changers Radio Show." Each week we interview leaders and give them an opportunity to tell their stories. Being an author gives people an edge in getting on our schedule. In fact, I became a co-host of this show because my partner on the air first invited me to be a guest on his radio show all because he saw my book!

In addition to traditional media, there are hundreds and thousands of blogs, podcasts, and video channels that interview experts all the time, and they too are starving for content. With a little bit of effort by you or a PR person, you could never run out of opportunities to demonstrate your expertise and promote you and your book!

Advantage #10: Association and Connection with Business Leaders and Celebrities

One of the great benefits of getting to speak and being interviewed by the media is the connections you make. Quite often, the host that interviews you will personally refer you to people in their network. When you share a stage, you often aren't a solo act, so you share the stage with other leaders and you inevitably make connections.

Being an author and hosting a radio show has placed me in a sandbox I wouldn't have been invited to play in otherwise. I've got a robust address book and network of colleagues that have been a boon to my business over the years – all because I decided to write a book in 2007.

Advantage #11: Reach Prospects and Places Advertising Could Never Get You and to Customers That Might Otherwise Ignore You

If you've been in the precarious position over the years of being a professional or business owner who could only generate prospects from paid advertising, you will be quite pleased with how things expand for you as an author.

I'm a big fan of advertising that works. Spend some money on an ad, generate leads, and make a few sales. It's a great system.

In my experience, and the experiences of the hundreds of clients I've worked with, advertising has limits. First of all, very few advertisements have longevity. That means you cannot use the same ad over and over for years. It certainly works in the short term, but whether it's a space ad in a trade journal, a Google Adword, or a postcard, you eventually see a diminishing return on your ads, and it forces you to change the message.

There's also the issue of reach. You can reach a lot of prospects online and through the mail, but the job of getting to some prospects is quite daunting. In my case, I work with CEOs and business leaders, and guess how much time they spend searching online or surfing Facebook? Zero. Have you ever tried to get the mailing address of a CEO or tried to get a piece of mail directly to a CEO without running it through an army of assistants?

Sometimes your only chance to reach your audience is when you're standing in front of them. Having a book allowed me to speak at conferences where my prospects were gathered for me. That's a huge advantage.

The other great thing is knowing that my targets often ignored or threw out deliberate advertising; the only thing I could get them to read of mine initially was my book. You might find the same to be true.

It would also be remiss to ignore the amazing resource we have with Amazon.com and BN.com. The reach and distribution of these behemoths are staggering, and can you not stop being downright giddy about the fact people go there to BUY?!

It doesn't take much to get your profile and materials into Amazon.com or Barnes and Noble's online store. You simply have to author a book. Having a printed book and an e-book available to sell at good prices to proven buyers is a gift from heaven. You are actually being paid to generate leads and raise your personal brand recognition!

Advantage #12: You Will Achieve Better Results from Your Advertising

I've discovered that marketing a book and using it in your sales process makes all your other advertising much more effective.

Case in point. When you get your book in a prospect's hands, you have a certain point of leverage now that you didn't before. That means your name carries some weight, and your prospects are consciously and subconsciously more in tune to your name.

When you send an e-mail, your prospect will see your name standing out from the dozens of messages in their inbox. When you send a letter or postcard, you will likely get it read. When you host a webinar or teleseminar, or even promote an upcoming speaking engagement and invite your prospects, they are more likely to attend.

As long as the information you are presenting is what customers want, and you are somewhat compelling in communicating it, you will maintain this advantage.

Here's another secret: Having made your prospects simply AWARE that you have a book raises their senses. They don't even need to have the book in their possession. You can talk about the book or show the book in your advertising as a credibility booster and get higher responses.

Advantage #13: Ads Capture Attention for Seconds ... Books Hold Attention for WAY Longer

In terms of a marketing asset itself, a book trumps many other forms of advertising media.

Ads will hold a prospect's attention for seconds or maybe minutes if it's compelling media, but nothing can match the attention you get from a book.

Even the most compelling stage presentation will last a couple of hours at most, but once that couple of hours is over and if you didn't get the lead or sale, you missed a chance. Your book can hold their attention for hours, days, weeks, and months.

Why?

Advantage #14: Books Have Longevity and Viral Power – Books Are Not Thrown Out, They're Valued

Books do not get tossed in the trash like sales letters or postcards.

Books don't get lost in a drawer like a common business card.

Books rest on shelves, desks, and countertops; in bathrooms (sorry, but true); inside backpacks; and now stored as electrons on an e-book reader.

Books have and always will have value. People just don't throw out books. They might get boxed up. They might get donated or given away, but they are very rarely, if ever, trashed.

Is there a better vehicle to deliver your message that is so widely valued and not disposed of within minutes?

Advantage #15: Books Are Cheaper Than Most Advertising When You Calculate Cost Per Lead

Later in the book I'm going to talk about a strategy that's made many people millionaires. It involves giving away copies of your book.

For some people, this seems like a foolish thing to do. Why in the world would you give away a book when you could be making ten to fifteen dollars a pop?

Simple – because I could make $10K, $100K, or more than a million bucks from just a single person getting my book. I don't know how much a client is worth to you, but I'm guessing a customer or client is certainly worth more than fifteen dollars.

Do a little math.

If your average client is going to be worth $10K to you over the course of twelve months, and it takes one hundred leads to generate a sale, would you be willing to give out one hundred copies of your book to land one client?

You might think your cost per book is $10, but in reality, it's more like $3.00. So to give away 100 books, you only have to invest $300. Maybe it costs you $5 to mail each book, so now your investment in 100 books becomes $800 with materials and mailing. How many times are you willing to spend $800 or even $1000 to get a $10K client? The correct answer is as often as you can!

Let's evaluate what you are doing right now.

Suppose you're a typical professional who is advertising in the local paper, with door hangers, or on the radio. Your call to action is usually an offer of a free consultation or free information. On average, you are probably getting a 1% response rate, which is still generous.

What if I told you that you could get a 5%, 10%, even 20% rate of response on an ad simply by switching your offer to be "get my book for free"? Now that's exciting.

What does that do to your average cost per sale when your 5x'ing or 20x'ing your lead flow, even if it costs you an additional $8 per lead to mail them a book?

To me, this is exciting math!

Advantage #16: You Leave a Legacy, You Obtain a Personal Achievement (Cross Off That Bucket List Item)– Or You Can Just Brag to Family and Friends (and Parents)

Maybe this is the most beneficial thing of all – bragging rights!

If you are like some entrepreneurs, your family has no idea what you do. In my case, I gave my parents copies of my books so they could both understand what I do for a living, as well as attempt to communicate it to their friends. For others, it's a professional rite of passage to get a book done. Whether it's an expectation or a necessity, whatever the case may be, it's something you need to stop putting off.

For the others, it's a bucket list item or a personal goal. Secretly, many people want to author a book, but a majority of the people won't act on it. You can be the small minority that chooses to act and achieve a great sense of pride.

The feeling of holding your book in your hands and searching for (and finding) your name on Amazon is a personal and professional achievement you can be proud of.

As with many of the clients I've worked with, leaving a personal and professional legacy may play a big part in your decision to author a book. You have great stories, experiences, and principles that you want others to remember you for.

I've given you sixteen undeniable advantages that give you a leg up on everyone else in your market just by authoring a book, yet you haven't taken this step. Why?

Bad Excuses for Not Getting a Book Done

Time for a little tough love.

You would love to gain the advantages of being an author over other mortal beings but have not taken the step (and it's a step, not a leap).

WHY NOT?

Here are the common excuses I've heard as a marketing consultant and business coach over the last ten years:

I Want to . . . I'll Get Around to It Someday

Maybe you will, but most likely you won't. It's never too late to get your book done, but it's always going to be later than you wish you had if you ever get it done. When you start to reap the benefits, you are going to wonder why you avoided this for so long!

I Don't Have Time

Right. You don't have time.

Do you have time to spend an hour on Facebook each day? Are you getting your two hours of television each night? Can't miss your weekly round of golf? Spending your working hours on "very important projects" that actually aren't that important at all, or could easily be done by someone else?

I'm no saint when it comes to time management. I'm probably a poor model for you to emulate. All I'm saying is that how we spend our time reflects our priorities, so until you resolve the importance of getting a book done, you will continue to put it off.

I Don't Know How

I get this. Sometimes you don't start a project because you don't know how.

So how did you figure out the skills to create a balance sheet? To fix a car? To diagnose a skin condition? To hit a baseball? To cook a gourmet meal? To draw a blueprint?

You learned. You read a book. You followed a teacher. You practiced. You started.

Just like learning to do the simplest of things or the most complex things, you make a decision to learn something, and you set out to learn. There is no shortage of places to learn how to author a book and get it published.

Of course, the other route we take when we don't know something is that we hire someone who does! We either try to fix that dishwasher ourselves or we call a repairman. We try to get up our own Google Adword campaign or we hire someone who can do it in his or her sleep. We set up our own website or we hire someone who will do it for us.

Getting a book done is no different from any other task you have in front of you. You either learn how to do it or hire someone who already knows.

I'm Not a Writer

This is a valid observation and certainly a good argument. I've worked with plenty of clients who hated to write but could speak for days on end.

Not being able to write is a roadblock in getting a book done, but it's not an excuse to stop trying.

Again, not being able to write to your satisfaction simply eliminates one option for you to get this done. There are many other ways to author a book other than you sitting down and hacking away on a word processor or scribbling a manuscript on a legal pad.

We'll talk about these options in a moment.

I Don't Know What to Write About

We're not talking about fiction books here where you must craft a great story. All we're talking about is crafting a book to convey knowledge you already posses, tell your unique story and connection to this knowledge, and in most cases, make a solid case for you or your company as a premier provider of products and services they desire.

If you have any sort of chops, any sort of skill, and any track record of experience, you will easily have enough to write about.

In most cases, you might develop a mental block because you are so close to the material and your story that it will take meeting with someone who has the ability to help draw out the book theme, purpose, structure, and content.

I personally did not realize the depth of my knowledge and experience when I wrote *Big Ticket eCommerce* in 2007. I was fortunate to have a book consultant working with me to draw out experiences, principles, and case studies that helped create a phenomenal book that has been well received by peers, prospects, and media.

I Don't Have a Publisher

You don't need a publisher. Self-publishing is the way to go.

Traditional publishing will not die, and there will still be publishing houses that take on authors and publish their books, but the days of an author having to create a manuscript and then peddle it to any publisher that will buy it are over.

I strongly support the self-publishing route and recommend it as the primary way for business authors to get their book into the hands of the public.

It's Too Expensive and Complicated to Hire This Out

Yes. It is expensive to have someone do this for you. It's like that in any industry. A can of paint costs $45 but hiring a painter to put it on the wall is going to cost $450.

I'm not saying that the outsourcing route or hiring someone to help you get your book done is right for you. I'll go over some considerations for you later in the book to help you decide, but this comes down to time and expertise. If time and your ability are working against you, then it's a great option to hire me and my experts to help you get your book done.

I've found that the best candidates for choosing the route of outsourcing their book project are those who have clients with healthy margins and revenue.

Professionals fall into this category for certain. Many financial professionals have clients easily worth $25K a year to them. Same with medical specialists whose patients might bring in $10K to $50K per procedure. Professional speakers who get paid $5K to $10K for a speech (or more) certainly are candidates. Other niche businesses like consulting or coaching can charge upwards of $100K for a single client over the course of a year or two.

The best way to make this decision is to say, "If I can land just one or two new clients from this book, it's paid for." If you can say this with confidence, then it's worth taking on the expense, especially when you are only required to put a little bit of time into the project and never have to sweat over the details.

Is a Book for Me?

I've developed a simple, non-scientific assessment to help you answer this question. If you're still reading this book, that's a pretty good assessment right there, but if you need further guidance, please consider some of these questions:

1. Are you the face of your business?

2. Do you have competitors who have good exposure?

3. Do you sell products or services that are somewhat complex, expensive, or have extended sales cycles?

4. Do you want to speak or be interviewed?

5. Would you consider your business to be "missional"?

6. Do you have case studies or experiences that could make good stories?

7. Are there frequently asked questions that you always have to answer?

8. Do you have the need or desire to personally brand

yourself or leave a legacy?

9. Do you want to record lessons you learned or communicate principles you want to pass on to others?

10. Do you have a "back-end" process to handle leads and inquiries?

11. Do you have a standard "call-to-action" that would easily translate to a book?

12. Do you have content that you can repurpose (blogs, articles, interviews, e-books, reports, etc.) or can you speak on your topic?

13. Do you have the need to create a new positioning in an established market or create a position in a new market?

14. Do you want to be a celebrity in your market?

15. Is writing a book on your bucket list or list of goals?

I won't ask you to tally your score and compare it to a chart. Simply, the more you find yourself answering "yes" to the questions above, the more ready you are to write a book, and the more a book will be an effective medium for you.

Maybe the best question of all is simply this: "Do you want to author a book?" If the answer is yes, then by all means, go do it!

Section 2

How to Get a Book Done

Where Do I Start?

Congratulations for making it this far in your decision process to get a book done! The first step in any journey is deciding to step out, and the next step is always the plan on how you will get there.

Before you take the journey of becoming an author, no matter how you execute it, you need to plan. There absolutely must be strategy, purpose, and direction to your book. It must also fit well into the bigger picture of your marketing and sales strategy.

When I begin to work with a client, one of the things I require is careful thought and assessment about their situation and current strategy. I also want to know about what they are intending to do and why.

Whether you are authoring your book yourself or hiring someone to do it for you, the following assessment in this chapter will be a thorough exercise and time well spent. Even if you don't decide to write a book, this assessment will force you to think about yourself and your business in a critical way, and it might even help you see things more clearly now than ever before.

I've been told by clients (who have hired me at premium rates) that this assessment was one of the most difficult, yet eye-opening exercises they ever did. Merely completing this assessment and getting to think about their business for a short time was worth more than they paid me.

I've included this assessment in this chapter, but I've also provided you a PDF and Word doc so that you can download it to your laptop and work inside the document itself.

Please visit http://www.MyBookDone.com/assessment and follow the instructions.

Ready?

The first step in getting your book done is getting to know you, your business, and your market. These questions and answers will help to hone in on your unique story and help you prepare the material that will be included in the book.

Do not rush through this. Take your time. Answer the questions as honestly and completely as you can.

There are a lot of questions that may seem redundant. That's okay; you don't need to answer every question. I may ask the same question a number of ways to help get you to think about all angles.

Okay, time for you to get to work!

Book Assessment

1. Why do you want to author a book?

2. What do you want your book to be about?

3. What's your origin story? Describe it as it relates to your career and business and where it fits into your book. Be sure to include points that are going to be helpful in creating a unique story for your offer/business.

4. Describe your business and how you feel your book fits into what you are doing or intend to do.

5. Who is the ideal reader of your book, and what would be his or her motivation to read it?

6. Who are your competitors in this space?

7. Who are your allies in this space?

8. What books about this subject are currently available at Amazon.com (or what keywords would you use to search these books out)?

9. Start a list of PRINCIPLES you would like to teach in

your book.

10. Start a list of CASE STUDIES, STORIES, and EXPERIENCES that prove the PRINCIPLES you intend to teach in your book.

11. Clearly and succinctly state the ACTION(s) you would desire readers to take after reading your book.

12. Describe the POSITIONING you intend for your book to create for you or your company.

13. State the specific MISSION or MESSAGE that you hope people catch and pass on after reading your book (if applicable).

14. Fill in the blank: "After reading my book, my readers will have learned more about _____ whether they ever contact me or not."

15. Start a list of TRAITS you want people to discover about you in your book.

16. Fill in the blank: "My biggest hesitations or fears about getting my book done (whether I do it myself or hire someone to do it for me) are _____."

17. Fill in the blank: "My ideal outcome for this book would be_____."

18. Which is more important to you in getting your book done, SPEED or SCOPE (do you want it done fast, or do you want to take as much time as you need to make it complete to your satisfaction)?

19. Fill in the blank: "I intend on getting my book done by_____." (*DATE*)

20. If you already have any working titles or chapter ideas in your head, get them into a document as soon as possible.

Start to make a virtual and/or physical file of all marketing materials that you've used recently. Include transcripts of webinars, speeches, or teleseminars. Also include any articles you've written and blog posts. You should also create a document listing important URLs to your business and book.

What Kind of Book Should I Write?

Your Book Structure

For the majority, the type of book you will be writing is a non-fiction book, targeted to a specific audience, with a defined call to action for the purposes of positioning, personal branding, and delivery of a unique message. Basically, it will help to grow your business and enhance your credibility.

You could choose to do an autobiography for the purposes of telling your story and establishing your personal brand. The book will be filled with experiences or life situations where you describe an experience and/or convey a life or business lesson (your principle) along with it.

Bill Gates, Steve Jobs, Richard Branson, Howard Schultz, and many more entrepreneurs like them have memoirs or biographies in print to both tell their personal story and convey their principles of success.

A twist on this type of book is a biography you author about someone else. This is where you tell someone else's story. There's also an anthology or compilation type of book where it's not just one person's story. Go to Amazon.com and search for "business biographies" and you'll see a large number of books by authors who are re-telling the stories of famous entrepreneurs and leaders and putting their own twist on it.

Another popular format that we all have read is the classic "how-to" book, where you will take on the role of a teacher leading the reader on the discovery of a topic or skill. A derivative of the "how-to" book is the FAQ book, where the entire goal is to inform the reader on the answers to common questions about a subject in a very direct format. There are thousands of business books that have a purpose of educating the readers on a theory or discoveries on a topical matter. Great books like *How to Win Friends and Influence People, Think and Grow Rich, Good to Great, The E-Myth* and many more fall into this category.

Bear in mind this type of book is trying to both educate the reader and offer them proof of the author's expertise. To get your potential customers to consider your products and services, you will want to include a healthy dose of case studies and proof that not only demonstrate your facts but also demonstrate your value and track record.

A less-likely format for a business book, but one you might consider anyway, is a journalistic-type book where you research a topic and report on it. You might also consider an exposé where you research a topic and present a case with a defined purpose in mind. There are also opinion or editorial books where you take a side of a story or a debate and make your case to the reader.

Obviously, there are no hard and fast rules. Your book could certainly contain elements of all these. It's important that you use the proper style of book to best convey your purpose to the reader.

Your Book Media

The term "book" is almost as generic as the word "album" these days. No longer does book mean just paper and ink.

I would encourage you to have the goal of producing a paper and ink book because it's extremely easy with the tools I'll share with you, but by no means should you limit yourself to one medium knowing your prospects will likely consume it in different ways.

Your choices today are hardcover, paperback, and electronic (written and audio).

As you know, Amazon.com sells more e-books these days than paperback and hardcover books. During the Christmas season of 2012, Amazon sold millions of Kindle devices and has plans to sell even more with aggressive pricing strategies. Given the number of Kindle devices, Nooks, iPads, tablets, and readers on smartphones, you cannot ignore the trend. Millions and millions of people own devices – you need to have that platform covered.

This has obviously turned the publishing world on its ear, and as authors, we need to adapt to our readers' habits.

My advice to a business author would be to produce a paperback book and a Kindle/Nook version to satisfy a majority of your audience of readers.

Hardcover books are more expensive to produce and sell. Although not a requirement, hardcover books tend to be longer than other books and carry a higher prestige. A great deal of published books by traditional houses launch books first as a hardcover, then once it hits a critical point, they offer a paperback. Quite simply, the publisher makes more money on hardcover books. That's why they do this.

Let's talk about e-books.

There are some great advantages to e-books:

- **They are easy to produce.** All you need is a word processer and the ability to save the document into an Adobe PDF format (most word-processing programs like Microsoft Word allow you to save in this format).

- **There are no size limits.** There's no limit to how short or how long an e-book can be. E-books can be three pages long or 3,000 pages long. Obviously, longer books become a problem when your file size starts to creep up, so don't go crazy.

- **They are easy to distribute.** When you generate a

PDF, you can e-mail it, put it on a website, burn it to a CD, print it on your printer, etc. It makes it very easy to distribute because 99% of computer users can open and read a PDF file.

- **They are easy to change and update.** When you print 500 books, you can't change the contents. Printing is final. E-books can be updated and re-distributed at any time. There is no cost for inventory or in re-distributing.

- **Kindle e-books allow you to sell your book on the greatest distribution channel on the planet.** Getting a book on Amazon.com and making it available to nearly five billion people around the world is unbelievable. The fact that millions of people (especially "wealthier" demographics) own a Kindle or use the app on their smartphones gives you a portal to deliver your message, unlike at any other time in human history. Remember, Kindle sales dwarf the sale of paper and ink books by a long shot.

E-books do have some disadvantages because they are so easy to produce and distribute:

- **They have a lower perceived value.** Sorry, we're

still in the days when people value physical over digital. There's something intimate about physically holding something versus just possessing something. Hugs and kisses from your children wouldn't be the same over Skype, would they? When I give someone my book (especially when I personally sign it), that's a genuine interaction with someone you can't get with an e-book.

- **They have lower consumption and interaction.** E-books are easy to lose on your computer or reader. You can collect a hundred e-books and never get around to reading them. They also don't scream at the reader "Read Me!" like if it was sitting on their desk. I've got dozens of e-books on my device that I've never even opened up. I just got them because they are free, cheap, or interesting.

- **Producing a Kindle book in the right format is a challenge, technically.** There are all kinds of software and people out there who can tackle this challenge for you at little or no cost, but it's a challenge nonetheless.

In a perfect scenario, you will have an e-book (both PDF and Kindle format) version available for your readers, as well as a paperback.

When we talk about marketing your book and getting new business, I prefer the paperback format because it's inexpensive to produce but highly perceived. It also allows me to physically put something in my prospect's hands, which, as we already discussed, is never thrown away. A paperback book has tremendous staying power and leverage for an author.

I always have books in my car for the instances when I run into potential clients. It trumps everyone at networking events who are just handing out normal business cards!

Self-Publish or Get Published?

I can speak to this first-hand, as I have both self-published a book and had a book published by Entrepreneur Press.

I'd much rather have a self-published book than a published book for many reasons:

- **Total control of distribution** – I don't have any restrictions on when or where I wish to bring my book in the marketplace, nor am I restricted on what price I choose to offer it at.

- **Self-published books can be completed in weeks or months** – My self-published book took about six months to complete, but my published book took about sixteen months. Red tape and administration are totally eliminated with your own book. This book in your hands right now took me about six weeks to complete because I had a great majority of the material produced from speeches, webinars, and articles.

- **All parts of the process can be outsourced** – Whatever you need help with – be it the writing, editing, design, or layout – all of it can be done with outsourced professionals you choose and hire at rates that are affordable. You are not limited to the resources provided to you by a publisher alone.

- **Higher royalties on any sales** – A publisher will pay advances to authors to get a book done, but take about 80 to 90% of the book's royalties. Self-published authors get paid 100% (noting that distributors like Amazon will still take 20 to 30%).

- **Amazon CreateSpace.com program** – The biggest advancement in self-publishing has been Amazon's self-publishing platform. They can assist you with every part of the publishing process, except for the writing. It allows you to hire service providers for various aspects of the process or do it all yourself. It gets the book from manuscript to published work in a matter of days, and you get to obtain copies of your books at a substantial discount over retail.

- **Complete freedom and ownership of content** – You are always at the whim of a publisher's editorial staff and standards. It will limit your ability to market yourself within the book and really gain the benefits you desire to grow your business. Self-publishing gives you complete control of every word in the manuscript as well as the layout and design.

What Is the Process for Writing a Book?

The major stages of authoring a book from concept to launch are:

Planning – The assessment I provided gives you the book foundation.

Outlining – Includes working titles and chapter ideas (not in any particular order).

Writing – Producing the manuscript!

Editing – Editing working drafts. Editing and writing is an iterative process.

Proofing – Dotting *i*'s and crossing *t*'s.

Designing – Including the interior, the front cover, spine, and back cover.

Reviewing – All aspects of the book, including a final read through and approval of design.

Publishing – Getting your book on Amazon.com and BN.com!

Planning

This is the stage where you decide what the book is about, whom it will target, and the purpose. The assessment I included in a previous chapter is your resource to get this done.

It is important that you take the assessment and write out your answers on a legal pad or working document. It will fire your brain into a creative mode, and reading back what you wrote is a key in creating an outline and initial draft.

Don't move on to writing a draft until you are satisfied with your planning!

Outlining

Part of the assessment asks you to start brainstorming working titles and chapter ideas. My suggestion is to take your time doing this and carry around a little notebook as ideas come to you over a period of days and weeks.

First of all, don't start with titles. If you spend all of your energy and mindshare on a title, you might never move forward. Good writers always have a very basic (and often poorly worded) working title and then focus on the outline.

You will certainly find that during the process of outlining, writing, and editing that a title will appear out of the cosmos. That's just the way it works.

I've seen authors write a title and then get stuck inside a box. It limited their writing, and the book's scope was too narrow or off target. Just pick a working title that is very general and move to chapter ideas.

Chapter ideas are not chapter titles. They are ideas. Think of chapters in your book as main points you want to cover. If you want to convey principles to your reader, then each chapter might be a principle. Perhaps you are teaching a process – each chapter would be a part of the process (as is the case with this book you're reading). In a biography, chapters might be points in time.

Brainstorm your chapter ideas on a white board, note cards, or legal pad. I'd say when you have fifteen to twenty, you are in good shape. In the end, you might end up with more or less, but you don't want to limit yourself here. Write down all the ideas or main points you want to cover in your book and write them down as chapter ideas.

One trick I've seen writers use is writing their ideas on index cards or Post-it notes. They write one chapter idea on each card. It helps them later in the process to organize the chapters.

That brings up one more word of caution. Don't determine the chapter order now. The order of the chapters might be obvious in some cases, but don't box yourself in with trying to get an order now. That can come later.

If you find you're getting stuck for ideas, one of the ways to juice your brain is to go to Amazon.com and search for books that are similar to the topic you are writing on and see how other authors have organized their main points. Just about every book on Amazon has the "Look Inside" feature. Use it – but don't plagiarize!

Before you start the writing process, it's a good idea to do a little editing on the chapters. Look at all your ideas. Are there some chapters that are very similar and could be merged into one? Are there some chapter ideas that seem out of place? Toss them aside.

Once you are comfortable with your chapter ideas, it's time for the big commitment . . . WRITING!

Writing

What happens in this stage is up to you. Whether you are outsourcing this work to a ghostwriter or tackling it yourself, this is obviously the most time-consuming and intense part of the process. This is where most authors get stuck, by the way. Many of you might have a half-done manuscript sitting on your hard drive right now!

There are volumes of books out there that will teach you how to write if you choose to do this yourself.

Let me offer you some tips on writing to help you finish a draft in a timely manner and not get stuck:

• *Thorough Planning*

I promise you, the more time and effort you put into the planning and outlining process, the easier it will be to write your first draft.

• *Scheduling*

Schedule your writing time like you would a meeting. Spending even just one hour a day writing will get you moving. DO NOT – I repeat – *DO NOT* save your writing time for the late evening after you've worked a full day, eaten dinner, and tucked the kids in. Your mind and body are tired, and you will not have the motivation or ability to write efficiently. I advise you to write in the morning when your mind and body are fresh.

As part of your scheduling, I suggest you plan each writing session by also noting which chapter you intend to work on. Once you reach your time limit or you plow through the chapter, put it away.

• *Don't Edit as You Go*

Writing a working draft isn't about finding the exact words or getting all the words spelled correctly. I'd even go as far as to tell you to turn off the spellchecker and just write.

Your goal is to get ideas and words from your head on to the paper (or screen). Do not edit in your head or on the screen. Let it flow!

• *Don't Write in Order*

You don't write a book by starting with "In the beginning . . ." or "Once upon a time . . . ." I suggest you begin writing section by section (or chapter idea by chapter idea). Pick a chapter idea that you know really well, one that you can start writing very easily. It will not only get your juices flowing, it will give you confidence. Then, working through chapter idea by chapter idea, you can make your way through the book.

• *Write the First and Last Chapter LAST*

After writing the meat of the book, you'll better know how to introduce the material in the first chapter, and conclude the book in the last chapter. Almost every author I know does it this way. It's smart because you have a better sense of how you will set up the reader to absorb your content and how you want to conclude, along with providing a strong call to coaction.

• *Drafts*

Your first draft is complete when you have all the chapters done. At this point, you can begin to edit the content, organize the chapters, create chapter titles, and start thinking about book titles.

All the editing is done by the writer at this point. I usually will start at the beginning of the book and work my way through. I run a spell check to get obvious errors taken care of, and then start reading and editing.

Don't get obnoxious over grammar, as that can be handled by your professional editor, but the goal of this stage is to go through the manuscript over and over until it meets your satisfaction. That means you are satisfied with the content and it connects with your book plan.

My suggestion is to have trusted colleagues or associates read the book. Maybe have your spouse read it if he or she understands your market, but definitely have someone read the manuscript who knows something about the material you are presenting. Take their feedback and make changes as appropriate.

This is an iterative process. I cannot tell you when you will be done, but I will encourage you to get it done. The worst thing you can do is edit the book to the nth degree so that it never gets published. Perfectionists – take heed: You will never be totally satisfied with the book. Never. Get over it. Set a deadline to have a final working draft done and submit it to the editor. Please.

A poorly written book will out-perform a book that never sees the light of day. Write a good book, but don't obsess.

Editing and Proofing

Do not skip or skimp on this. Hire a professional editor and proofreader. They will not break the bank. Don't hand off your manuscript to a high school student who loves English class!

The talents of a professional editor and proofreader will make your book shine! Editors who are skilled will help discover holes in your manuscript that need to be filled, rough sections that need to be reined in, and redundant content that can be made more efficient. And if you forgot those pesky grammar rules the day you graduated high school, your editor can help you fix any errors you make.

You should expect your editor to read the book on two levels – for grammar and for clarity. Even if he or she knows nothing about the subject, the editor will have the skills to challenge you to make the book the best it can be.

At this point, you should also have your title done. I really like the *Title: Subtitle* format.

For instance, the full title of my book is *Big Ticket eCommerce: How to Sell High Price Products and Services Using the Internet*. Note the title is catchy, and the subtitle describes exactly what the book is about.

I'd recommend that if you can't come up with a title, that you go with a subtitle. What I mean is don't try and get too cute with a title if you can't find something that works.

What's more important to me as a marketer is that my title conveys exactly what the book is about and contains rich keywords that can come up when people search on Google and Amazon.com.

Designing

Laying out the interior of your book from an electronic document is quite complex from the standpoint of 99% of us, but a book designer can do this in her sleep. There are dozens of standards and stipulations when it comes to laying out and printing a book – even if you self-publish – so under no circumstances should you attempt this yourself.

I would encourage you to visit **CreateSpace.com** and read about the various book sizes and layout options so you can help the designer make the right choices for your book, but do not do this yourself. The first time you try to get page numbers correct, you will take years off your life!

Same with designing the colors and graphics for the front cover, spine, and back cover. You will want to find a professional that does this as well. What they will require from you are color choices and graphics choices.

I usually give the designer a color palette and the theme of the book, and I get three options back for my review. I pick one and make any suggestions to make it what I want. The best way to do this is to provide your designer some actual book covers to model. Even the best designers hate a blank canvas.

Something very important that is 100% your responsibility is for you to tell the designer exactly what you want on the cover, especially the back cover.

I like to include a compelling, short narrative about what the book is about. I also want to print a bulleted list of main benefits that the reader will get when reading the book so that I can capture their attention. Lastly, you want to be sure you include a short author bio and, if you want, your picture.

Finally, I would highly suggest you put both a website URL and a phone number on the book. If your prospect never cracks the seal on the book, he or she can still find a way to contact you because what they need is right on the cover (making this the world's best business card)!

Reviewing

CreateSpace.com requires you to approve a "proof copy." You can do this online, but I absolutely insist you order a printed proof copy. I would highly suggest reviewing every single letter of the cover to be sure everything is correct. Then open the book and just leaf through it page by page and make sure each page is centered, the chapters start on the right hand side of the spread, the page numbers are correct, the margins are sufficient, and everything looks correct.

When you self-publish, you can always make changes at any time, but I prefer to at least check one more time before ordering 100 or more books!

Publishing

CreateSpace.com is the place I prefer to publish my book. There are awesome videos and tutorials that hold your hand through the entire process. If you follow their tutorials, you will have no trouble. Make sure you pay for the Expanded Distribution option. It only costs a few bucks, but it gets your book in more places and gets you higher royalties on all sales!

When you hit "Publish," it's a rush!! Celebrate your achievement, and usually within one to two days, you will see your book listed on Amazon.com. Celebrate again!

A Note on Finding Good People to Help You

You might be wondering about how to find experts to help you with various aspects of the book. If you don't choose a full service option like my company offers, the best way to find writers, editors, and designers is by taking advantage of the paid options on CreateSpace.com – or the way I've built my extensive team by combing through sites like Craigslist.org, Fiverr.com, Odesk.com, and author forums.

Before you hire a single person, get samples of their work and verify they actually produced the materials they send you.

Don't hire someone just based on price. Balance price and demonstration of ability.

At the end of this book, I'll make a few recommendations for you of people I've vetted. Understand that people move in and out of this industry, and their level of quality and commitment can change on a dime. You have to proceed with caution, and sometimes you get burned. That's just part of the game when you hire someone for project work, no matter if you are hiring a web designer or someone to paint your house. The key to not getting a raw deal is to make sure you get references, review samples of their work, get a referral, or thoroughly review their website. Being thorough in your decision will avoid most troubles.

Marketing Your Book

Marketing your book presents the same challenges as marketing your products, services, and personal brand. Just like marketing your business is not the same as selling, marketing a book is not about selling your book. In fact, the number of "rich" business authors in the world is very small, indeed.

Most become rich from their business first and then are asked to write a book to enhance their reputation and create more personal brand presence. Others get rich by hitting the speaking circuit and earn money by collecting speaking fees or selling products from the stage.

The truth of the matter is that you need to get rid of the notion that your primary marketing objective for your book is to sell it. Don't get me wrong, selling books is really fun, but it's not the primary objective.

Your goal in writing your book is to leverage it for greater opportunities. For some it might be speaking engagements, for others it might be product sales, and for you it might be getting more clients. Always make sure you make your objective about the book itself.

It's always imperative to me when I work with an author who is not writing a legacy book to make sure he or she has what we call a "back end." Humor aside, a back end is simply a term that means you have a higher income-generating product or service that you desire to offer your prospects. A book becomes another resource in your marketing funnel to lead them to your back-end offer.

That means you need to offer your readers, on top of great content and readability, a clear and direct call to action within your book. Even if they don't ever read a word, it needs to be clear to the person who is aware of your book what they need to do next.

Obviously, you are reading this book to discover the process of getting a book done. I've gone into a lot of detail about the entire process of getting a book published, including why you should do it and how you go about doing it. What you should also be keenly aware of at this point is that my "back-end" business and objective for this book is to get more clients so that I can help them produce a book. Along the way, I've demonstrated my knowledge in this area, and I've given you value and information that helps you learn more about the process and gives you the tools to both get a book done and strategize how you will use it. As you keep reading, you'll discover even more, and I'll continue to demonstrate value and my expertise in this area.

When you produce your book, you will need to do the same. Make sure your book informs, educates, and sells. It's all about the next step in the process and calling out to the people that are ready to move to the next step.

With that in mind, when you have a back-end business that you are looking to keep full of clients, it makes sense to me that an author's primary objective is not to SELL a lot of books, it's to GIVE AWAY a lot of books.

I've made a lot of people upset over the years who are adamant they will not give their book away. They cannot fathom taking something that costs $12.95 or $24.95 and giving it away. In my opinion, they are narrow minded and missing the point.

I'm convinced that once you understand that the back-end is the money-maker, you'll soon be looking to give away books to everyone you can! This is especially true when you realize that the actual cost of a book wholesale to you is usually around $3 for a paperback.

Many of you wouldn't flinch at buying clicks from Google or Facebook for $2 to $5.

CLICKS!!!

Not even a prospect. Simply a website visitor. Does it make sense that you wouldn't bat an eye spending $500 on 100 website visitors, but you have reservations giving away 100 books to prospects for $300?

What is more valuable, a person sitting on a website, taking seven seconds to look at your landing page, or a person sitting in their office or living room with a 150-page book you wrote? You know the answer.

I urge you to affix your mind to the thought process of

being generous with giving your book away and getting as many prospects as possible to hold the most valuable marketing asset you've ever produced in their hands.

In the next chapter, I'm going to reveal 21 actual ways I've worked with clients in giving their book away to generate prospects for their back-end business. I hope you enjoy it.

21 Ways to Grow Your Business by *Giving Away* Your Book

If you happened to flip right to this section, I encourage you to go back just one chapter and read about my philosophy on why you should give your book away. It's controversial but effective.

If you give away your book, it's a great way to market your book and fill your business with clients and prospects!

Give it away as a business card

I love this strategy. A book is the best business card on the planet. Nothing is sweeter than going to a networking function where everyone else is handing out ordinary business cards, and you are handing out signed copies of books (with your ordinary business card as a bookmark).

This often leads to more people coming to you. They'll be talking across the room and see people walking around with your book. They'll ask around and figure out where you are and go get a copy for themselves.

If you are like me, you have a drawer full of business cards. Attend any networking function, business conference, or meeting – everyone exchanges cards. I'm not saying this is wrong, but when you can give them **The World's Best Business Card**, do you think it's getting shoved in a drawer?

Your "card" will be sitting on their desk, table, or in their car for a while. It will be a daily reminder to them of who you are and that they need to see how they can work with you!

Give it away on your website as a lead-gen offer

If you've done any direct marketing on the Internet, or perhaps placed offline ads in publications, you know the strategy of giving away something in exchange for a person's contact information. We call this lead-generation advertising, or lead-gen.

Oftentimes the free gift is a white paper, an e-book, a DVD, a CD, or an audio MP3.

Having a book as your free gift is a great way to provide value to your potential leads! Take a look at one of my websites where I give away my book *Big Ticket eCommerce*. You can view the offer at http://www.FreeBigTicket.com.

Notice that I ask them first for their name, e-mail address, and phone number, then move them directly to an order page. I only ask the customer to pay shipping and handling, so I make no money on this transaction. I liquidate my lead cost and get a prospect for free.

Just know that you don't have to charge shipping and

handling. You can simply mail books to anyone that wants one, but I've found that by asking for a small amount of money, like $4.95, I get a better prospect. You should test and find out if that's the same for your market.

Give it away to secure appointments

I've seen this strategy used by many professionals who advertise free, in-office appointments:

"Just by showing up, you will get a gift valued at $14.95!"

It's a great strategy if you are already getting appointments but have had issues with people showing up. By ethically bribing them, you get greater compliance.

Hey, I've even seen churches use this strategy!

I visited a couple of mega-churches in the Chicago area, and one of the things they've offered me in exchange for my name and address and phone number after the service was . . . a free book!

It's highly effective at getting people to provide you with their name and address, and it's very valuable at helping people keep an appointment.

I'd suggest making the book part of your advertising so that the prospect's first "hurdle" with you is about the book, not about them hiring you for a premium service.

Give it away to editors of newspapers, blogs, and magazines to get interviews or articles

This is a targeting strategy that works well at getting you into places where your audience gathers, plus you'll get credibility by getting interviewed by authoritative media.

What you want to do is identify the media and publications that you desire. Find out the name of the blog owner, editor, or reporter who makes decisions and send them a personal letter along with a copy of your book.

Don't just ask for an interview. Remember, these individuals are charged with entertaining and educating an audience. They want to interview experts on subject matters their readers care about. Therefore, you want to offer them subject areas you can discuss with expertise. You want to let them know your take on current issues your market is talking about. You want to offer a lot of value and offer yourself up as a resource – solve a problem for these folks. They know you want to be interviewed, so you need to put on your sales hat and sell them as to why they should interview you.

In my experience, the book creates a "thump factor." It certainly stands out from e-mail, faxes, and social media messages. It also leaves the lasting impression on the individual that you actually cared enough to give them a valuable gift.

Give it away to book reviewers

There are book reviewers with publications offline and online. The purpose of these publications is to provide media outlets, libraries, institutions, booksellers, and publishers information about books.

Some of these reviewers charge you a fee for inclusion, some do not. I suggest that you try to get some free reviews, and also get some paid reviews if part of your strategy is getting your book out there in a significant way. Although this is not my favorite strategy, it does work for some people to get book sales moving.

Here are some sites you can visit. I don't have a formal relationship with any of these sites nor am I making any recommendation. I'm just providing you some shortcuts to get started and make a decision on your own.

http://www.bookreviewdirect.com/
http://www.bookreviewers.org/
http://www.midwestbookreview.com/
http://www.palmettoreview.com/
http://chantireviews.com/
http://www.booksneeze.com/
http://www.readerviews.com/
http://www.frontlist.com/

Give it away to radio show and podcast hosts for interviews

Just like newspapers, blogs, and magazines, radio show hosts need guests for their listeners.

I host "The Game Changers Radio Show" on AM560-WIND in Chicago, and we have had a number of authors on our show simply because they sent us a book with a compelling cover letter.

They informed us of their desire to be interviewed, gave us topical areas they could discuss, and most importantly, sent us a signed copy of their book as a "thank you in advance."

Give it away to promoters that host events and get speaking gigs

I love speaking in public, especially when the audience is filled with prospects. In my career, nothing has been more lucrative than using my book to get speaking gigs that led to client engagements.

The strategy is quite obvious. You identify events or people that host events where you want to speak. You send your book via UPS or FedEx to these promoters, and just as you would with a newspaper editor or radio show host, you let them know your desire to speak, and what areas of interest you can speak on.

Remember, no matter what the strategy, you always want to focus your pitch on what you can do for the promoter and their audience. Even if you don't get an immediate speaking engagement, you at least started a relationship that you can nurture, and you will eventually get on stage.

Give it away to clients as gifts

This is a great method to create a bond with your clients. You can thank them for their loyalty and patronage, and it creates a great excuse for you to reach out to them and say HEY!

This might give you an opportunity to celebrate face-to-face with your clients – don't just mail the books out! If you are a local professional, you can even host a book launch party for all your clients and give out the book as a party favor.

Give it away to list owners to get a teleseminar or webinar gig

Remember that a teleseminar or webinar is just a speaking engagement with a different stage.

The goal of a teleseminar or webinar might be to generate revenue, so you need to create a relationship with the host to find out what his or her expectations are.

In some cases, I've done teleseminars where I've pitched my services, but I've done others where I've given away my book. I actually prefer to do the latter because I can generate more leads for my business and start a relationship with them versus a one-off pitch for a premium service or product I'm offering.

Give it away as a bonus with a product or with your services

This makes sense. You can offer your book as an add-on bonus that helps sweeten the deal for things you are already selling.

Some of you sell CDs or DVDs with a workbook. You can throw your book in to add value to the offer.

If you offer a service like weight loss consultation, you can offer your book as part of the curriculum.

If you do taxes, you can offer your book to tax return clients.

It's a nice value gift for someone as a bonus for doing business with you.

Give it away as a Kindle book to get viral traction

Amazon has a service called Kindle Direct Publishing:

https://kdp.amazon.com

As part of this service, you have the option of offering your book for free for up to five days. If your book is good and people love it and review it, it could firmly place you in a great spot in Amazon's search results, and once the book is no longer "free," you can start to see sales and royalties.

The key, of course, is to have good content that people will want to review and recommend to other people.

Give it away at speaking events where you are not selling

If you speak at a networking event, association, trade group, or business event, and you are not allowed to directly sell your services from the stage, you should craft an offer that gets people to get your book easily.

You could do this by having copies in the back of the room, or you could collect business cards and mail out the books. Personally, I like to get the business cards and mail the book because it gives me a chance to include a letter and personalized offer.

One good hybrid strategy is to have a small number available to sign and give away at the event. You could do a contest and collect business cards and draw out the winners. Then, when you get back to the office, you mail out a copy of the book to the rest of the people as well.

Sneaky, but smart.

Give it away as a reward for sticking around for a presentation

Much like the example above, you could make copies of your book available to people for sticking around for an entire stage presentation, teleseminar, or webinar.

What I like to do is let people know that at the very end of the presentation, I'm going to offer them a free gift if they stick around. I don't reveal that it's a book until the end.

If your gift for sticking around has no value, people won't appreciate it. By now, you know the value of a book and the perceived value people place on it. A book is a perfect gift that people won't be upset they waited around for.

Give it away to associations and trade group leaders

These groups love great content that helps their members. You have to be very careful not to be pushy about this. If the leadership detects that your only motive is to circumvent them and get to members to poach them, then you won't get in the door.

It's important you go in with an education and service mindset and give compelling evidence that you would be a resource to them.

What you are looking to achieve beyond a level of trust is an opportunity to speak at their conference, contribute an article to their newsletter, or perhaps do a webinar for their members.

Many associations are receptive to authors who can provide valuable, educational, and compelling content to their members.

Give it away to prospects who respond to an advertisement

A great lead-generation strategy is to offer a copy of your book to prospects who show interest in you.

Whether you place an ad on the radio, space in the newspaper, or mail a postcard, instead of offering a traditional response piece, you want to offer a book that has a much higher perceived value.

It's important that the offer in your advertisement is strictly about the book, not about anything else.

If your book is about tax-saving strategies, your ad will be something like, "If you are tired of paying hard-earned income to the IRS and want to learn legal ways to cut your tax bill, then go to my website to request my new free book, *Secrets the IRS Doesn't Want You To Know.*"

That's just one example, but note that the end goal of this author's strategy is to get a tax client, but the ad never mentions that. It may not even mention who you are! But you do know that if someone requests a book, they at least have some interest in learning ways to keep the IRS away. These leads become prospects for the tax business.

Remember, the ad is about tying into the desires of the potential prospect, not about trying to sell them on you.

Give it away as a thank-you gift to clients – give two and ask them to re-gift it to someone they know

I love this strategy.

- Everyone likes a gift, especially when they don't expect it.

- Most people will gladly refer you if given the chance.

Let's combine these actions by offering a gift of TWO books to a client. You will send the books (or deliver them in person). You will take an opportunity to thank your client for their business, and then ask them a favor. Simply ask them to give the book to someone they know who might benefit from it.

First of all, they will love that you gave them a copy of your book, especially if it's personally signed to them. They will also be glad to hand your book to someone they know because of your great service to them.

Most professionals rely on referrals as the lifeblood of their business. You might actively ask your clients for referrals on a regular basis. Many might be reluctant to offer up names to you but would not mind handing your book to a friend. Better than a business card or a CD, a book has the credibility and value that supersedes any other gift you could offer your clients to hand out for you.

I had a financial services client who utilized this thank-you gift strategy over Thanksgiving. He mailed out forty books to twenty clients, and within a few days booked a client that will be worth $10,000 a year to him for many years. That's exciting!

What other "excuses" can you come up with to give away your book as a thank you to a client and get them to gift it to someone they know?

Give it away when you do interviews or write articles

When I contribute articles to publications or do interviews on the radio, I like to include a free book offer to the readers and listeners. Usually, the radio host will ask you to "plug" something. Having an offer of a free book is way more effective than just giving out a phone number or website address.

When you create an article for a publication, you will be

given a chance in a byline to state your name and contact info. I always promote a free copy of my book with a web address for people to go to get it.

This is a great way for you to create an opportunity for someone who is listening to you or reading your article and who wants more info to get that need satisfied right away. Sadly, if you don't offer them that opportunity, they will forget about you within minutes.

Give it away to libraries and institutions

If your book is something that contributes to a general audience, it's likely libraries and colleges would want it available to their constituents. Make it very easy for them to do this by meeting with the head librarian and offering a few copies of your book.

They may even suggest you host a talk or seminar if the topic has broad appeal.

Give it away as a requirement for new clients to read

I've seen professionals include their book as part of their service offering.

The book likely provides a foundation of knowledge that you need your client to have in order for you to provide the best service. It can save you from repeating yourself over and over, and it can set your clients up for success.

Your book can also be seen as a "philosophy" for your clients. For example, if you serve people as a group (as in a coaching program), it's important that they all have a base of knowledge or certain mindset. Your book can serve to get people to that place.

Give it away to sell your coaching/consulting (this is the workbook you will take them through)

Much like the example above, you may decide your book is best used as a textbook or workbook. You could choose to include study questions at the end of each chapter or include exercises for the reader to do.

You might then set up your consulting or coaching around your book and take your clients through the material. This is very much like a school environment that people are very comfortable and familiar with.

Give it away to powerful or famous people you want to meet

Who do you want to meet today?

It's very hard to pick up the phone and meet anyone you want. The more famous or powerful the person, the greater their defense shield against intruders will be.

Your job is to penetrate that defense system with the right strategy.

If you can get the mailing address of the person you want to meet, it's very easy to FedEx or UPS your book to them personally. Even if the person's assistant is screening mail, the "thump factor" of your delivery will get you on the top of the pile.

Depending on the person and the situation, you might choose to include a letter and ask that they call you, or you might send a letter and let the recipient know a day and time you will call them. I like the latter because, as we know, everyone is busy.

When you call, you can let the assistant know you are the person that mailed a copy of your book. At the very least, it will identify you and get a conversation with the schedule keeper; at best, they will patch you through to the person you want to talk to.

In essence, your book is simply a key to unlock a door or get you past the velvet rope. What happens next is up to you!

Give it away through referral partners in their places of business

Here's a great strategy to get people to refer you:

Suppose you're a chiropractor and you want to attract

people from the community. You wrote a book entitled *Secrets to Reducing Stress and Staying Healthy.*

You could work out an arrangement where a professional service provider or a local merchant – such as a spa, car wash, restaurant, or health food store – would display your book. Maybe you have to work out a reciprocity arrangement or commission for referrals, but again, if the book is a valuable resource, people won't immediately decline your request to display it.

Give it away in obvious places where your prospects might run into it

This builds off the previous idea, but let's expand on this.

Many people are placing Facebook ads these days to drive traffic to their websites because you can target groups of people that are likely interested in your services.

A free book offer on Facebook to your targeted prospects can significantly outperform a standard ad where you drive them to your website. I've seen many great ads targeted to me personally while on Facebook.

For example, I'm interested in baseball and coaching, and I've seen an ad offering me a free book on coaching youth baseball! I've seen my share of marketing books, of course, being that's my business, and also about how to market a book!

But you can be creative without spending money on advertising!

Suppose you are a dermatologist. You write a book about ways to protect yourself from the sun and still have a great day at the beach. Do you think you could pass out a few copies at . . . the beach?

If you are a fitness instructor and you work at a club where they want you to drum up private fitness clients, what better opportunity is there than to pass out a book to members of the club and get more clients?

If you run a sports-performance clinic, you'd want to have your book at tournaments where they gather dozens of teams in a weekend.

Get the picture?

You need to be in places with your book where your prospects will cross your path.

Give the book away at business meetings

I want to encourage you to make it a personal rule to have a signed book available any time you have a business meeting with someone you're meeting for the first time. Even if you don't have any intention of doing business with the person, you never know who they know! Making a great first impression is key to networking, and providing a gift of your book is always a great first impression.

Give the book away at business conferences

If you are keeping track, we're actually on idea number 25! As you can imagine, there are going to be 25 more ways you can think of to give your book away for free, and I encourage you to do so!

In terms of business conferences, I know it's impractical to fly or drive to a business conference with a box of books. If you know you'll be at a conference where there are 500 or 2500 people that are likely prospects, you will want to meet as many people as you can!

One thing you want to do is make sure you have at least some books on hand to give to people you develop good rapport with. You know, the ones that you end up having meals or drinks with. You can squeeze a dozen or two books in your suitcase for sure.

You obviously want to meet more than a dozen people and get them your book, so you will need to get a little creative.

I've done two things that work well. First, I have created two-sided, full-color business cards. On one side is my standard contact info, and on the back side is a free offer.

Here is one version I've used with success, which advertises a free video seminar on how to become a published author:

I've also used an oversized card with either my book cover or a promotional ad on the front, and then on the back I've mimicked what I have on my business cards. I hand those out to as many people as I can meet, and if I feel they are a great connection or good prospect, I will let them know I have some copies available in my room, and then I set up a time to get them a copy.

What you want to do, once again, is leverage your book as the bait, appeal to the wants of your prospects, and make the initial connection be about the book.

The Professional Services and Consulting Strategy (aka The Million Dollar Business Strategy)

In the previous chapter, I talked about ways you can market yourself by giving away your book.

I want to expound on one strategy that involves giving the book away but also covers your costs in the process. I have personally used this strategy to sell multiple five-figure consulting deals over the years, and implemented this strategy for clients who have turned it into hundreds and thousands of dollars in their business, and some are turning it into millions.

Obviously, just giving a book away will not guarantee you anything. I have no idea what your business is or what your skills are in making sales. What I am saying is that if you have the right market, offer, skill set, and sales process, using this strategy might be a game changer for you.

Here's the strategy:

1. Create business cards, ads, and postcards with a Free Book Offer and drive them to a website or toll-free recorded message. The goal is to get them interested

in obtaining a free book.

2. The website or recorded message gives the person instructions on how to get their free book — either by filling out a form or leaving the information on the recording that "sells the free book" but requests $4.95 for shipping and handling. We do this to liquidate our costs, for one, but most importantly, we get a better prospect. We have an excuse to collect full contact information, and by virtue of the prospect using a credit card, we know the level of interest and commitment is much greater. I would suggest that on the webpage where you are collecting their information that you first get their name and e-mail, then have a second step where you get the rest of the information.

3. Mail them the book in a package sent by first-class mail or priority mail.

4. On the day you mail the book, call them and let them know the book is on the way. You want to e-mail them as well, but it's the personal connection that will surprise them. I strongly suggest you have your assistant do this or hire someone to do this for you. If you make the call, you risk letting the prospect

think you are always available. It doesn't establish boundaries between you and your prospects, which I believe is important. You also don't want to be tempted to sell, and you don't want to give the chance for the prospect to get a free consultation . . . yet.

5. On Day 3, have your appointed person call the book buyer and ask them if they received their book. Again, do not sell, do not try to push the prospect into anything. Allow the prospect to request an appointment with you, but you should never suggest it on this call.

6. On Day 7, have your appointed person call them again and find out how they liked the book and if they had questions. The caller is not equipped to answer any questions other than the logistics of them getting the book. Any question the prospect has is an opportunity for them to talk with YOU. If the prospect has any questions at all, have the appointed caller let the prospect know that because they have received the book, it entitles them to a BONUS FREE consultation with you. Have the appointed caller set up an appointment on your schedule for a fifteen- to twenty-minute consultation. Only work with

appointments, never rely on the person calling you back or you calling them later in the day. I believe appointments are professional, and people are more likely to take appointments seriously.

7. Once you get the prospect on the phone for a consult, you now have the opportunity to work them through your sales process.

Case Studies

I have set up a page online that features some clients I've worked with and their books. I encourage you to visit and learn about real people I've helped to become published authors.

http://www.mybookdone.com/client-success-stories.php

Bryan Sullivan of Vellum Financial is a Certified Financial Planner and uses his book constantly in a number of ways to drive new clients to his practice. Bryan especially loves my "Thank-You Strategy" and gets new business by giving *two* copies of his book to potential clients, giving the client an opportunity to gift the book to someone they believe it will benefit.

Anna Lee Leonard is also a Certified Financial Planner and Radio Host who loves the response her book is getting from clients and prospects alike. Her life story and her business mission are captivating, and her book gave her the perfect platform to tell her story and make important connections to her clients.

Doug Anderson is a Local Marketing and Business Consultant who needed a resource to set him above the crowd of consultants reaching out to local business owners. Doug has a lot of interesting strategies that he revealed in his book about how to drive customers to your door.

Mark Imperial is a DJ/Entertainer who wrote a book along with eighteen other DJs aimed at educating brides and couples about how to create the perfect wedding reception. Mark taught these DJs how to use the book to get more appointments and gigs!

If you think real hard, most professionals, consultants, coaches, speakers, service providers, and retailers could easily come up with enough material for a book and figure out ways to drive clients and customers to their door.

For instance, I have a friend who has self-published five books and leveraged the books into lucrative speaking engagements with a large CEO organization, and also to build up a six-figure executive coaching practice.

I worked with a Life Coach who used a self-published book to attract $10,000 coaching clients on a consistent basis.

I've worked with an entrepreneur who serves parents of children with dyslexia. He wrote a book and gave it away to help attract attention to a software program he developed to help these children increase their ability to read and comprehend.

I've worked with an individual who launched an information marketing business in a blue-collar industry using his book.

I've worked with a yoga instructor who used her book to tell her personal story of achieving wellness and healing to add a foundation and differentiating factor for her business.

I've worked with an individual who is a leading consultant in the online conversion space who needed to create a personal brand to set himself up with a higher caliber of clientele.

I have many more client examples and strategies to share with you.

I specifically offer a consultation package that allows you to discuss book ideas with me and specific strategies on how you will use the book to drive new clients and customers into your business.

I would encourage you to call my office at 1-877-349-2615 and inquire about a Book Plan and Consultation, or visit http://www.MyBookDone.com

If you have a valid book idea and business need, I will be glad to work with you to develop a book idea and plan, plus decide on which strategy would be best to meet your goals.

Get Your Book Done in Three to Nine Months with My Team

I'd be a poor teacher if I spent this entire book teaching you how to use a book to sell your services and not tell you about how you can work with me! The process of getting a book done on your own is quite doable, as you now know, but for some of you, it makes more sense to outsource 95% of the work to someone that can get it done faster because it's what they love to do. So if you believe this is something that might be of interest to you, please read on. If not, just read through as an opportunity to look at the process you might take if you do this on your own.

Phase 1: Book Plan and Consultation

The My Book Done Plan and Consultation is the foundation for getting your book done, whether you move forward with the My Book Done Service or you choose other options.

Our first step in getting your book done is getting to know you, your business, and your market. These questions and answers will help to hone in on your unique story and help you prepare the material that will be included in the book. You will first need to complete a Book Assessment (sent to you as a Word doc). Once this form is complete, you will send it to me and set up a phone call.

The assessment serves as a foundation for our book plan interviews. It is during these calls that we brainstorm book ideas and decide on an objective for the book, theme, and key points to cover. These interviews are recorded so that any great comments or ideas from you are preserved. In my experience, some golden moments occur in these interviews.

From these two key milestones, I will put together a set of interview questions to ask you if you plan on moving forward with the My Book Done Service. These are the questions that you provide detailed answers to for the meat of your book.

We'll likely have one scheduled phone call to review the assessment and give me the opportunity to clarify any questions I have. After the first phone call, I will prepare a draft Book Plan and send it to you, and we'll get on the phone again. We'll work through and finalize the plan. If we need to do more work, we'll continue offline and schedule a third call if needed. Once the Book Plan is completed to the satisfaction of both of us, you will have the plan in place to start on your book.

Phase 2: Interview Process

The interviews are scheduled for a time when you are most

comfortable and energetic. It's important that you are rested and not distracted. I find that mornings are best for most people. You should not have cell phones nearby, e-mail open, or potential visitors walking in (like kids, staff, or service people). You need to be focused and have high energy.

The interview takes place over the phone, and we connect to you via Skype. This allows us to easily record the call. If you have Skype, we will ask for your contact details, or we'll call you using Skype's call-to-phone feature.

Each interview usually lasts between 75 and 90 minutes. Don't worry if your interview runs shorter or longer than this time. This represents an average for most interviews. We'll pace the interview for your book, not anyone else's. If you need a break during the interview, we can pause the recording.

In most cases, we will schedule multiple interviews so that we don't go into a marathon mode. This will ensure good quality for the entire interview.

You will receive a digital copy of your interview (and pre-interview) in case you want to use them for other marketing purposes.

Once each interview is complete, the audio of your interview is sent to a transcriber who gets the entire interview down into written words. You will get a copy of that as well.

We will usually get our interviews completed within two to six weeks based on each other's schedules.

Phase 3: Writing

This is the key phase of the project, for obvious reasons. We will take the audio interview and written transcription and send it off to a ghostwriter.

Don't be alarmed, this person is alive and well and is not just interested in writing horror novels. Ghostwriters are plentiful throughout the world, and believe it or not, many notable authors use ghostwriters, and most of your biographical books are penned by a ghostwriter.

These talented individuals take the words you speak and turn them into a manuscript. They do not take any copyright, and they are not given credit within the book. Your readers will never know your book was written by another writer. Remember, it's not who writes the book, it's who authors it. You are the author of the book, and most of the words and all of the concepts within the book are your own. The writer has the ability to formulate your words into a seamless manuscript that is 100% in your own voice.

This process can take thirty to ninety days, depending on the book. It all depends on the writer's availability and the complexity of the material. It also depends on how much good material we are able to provide him or her within the interview. This is why all the steps leading up to this point are so critical.

This process involves writing outlines, chapter titles,

working titles, drafts, and re-writes. It's a lot of back-and-forth between the writer and me, but it's all meant to produce the best-quality manuscript possible. This seems like a "dead period," but believe me, there's work being done.

This is the point when we may need to get back on the phone to fill in any gaps in the content. Sometimes when writing the book, we'll find some information missing or need to insert a story or more content on a subject, so we'll get back on the phone and record that. It's all in the spirit of having the best book possible!

During this time, you will need to get some things together. We will need a bio, a high-resolution head shot, and customer testimonials. You may also choose to ask someone to write the preface of your book. This can be (and usually is) done by someone with some prominence in your market: a customer, a business associate, or someone that can set your book up for the readers. We'll discuss this more when we're into the process.

Phase 4: Proof and Editing

Once we settle in on a draft we're both comfortable with, you will get to review it and offer any constructive criticism. These suggestions will be dealt with and handled by the writer as necessary.

Once we both agree on the manuscript, it's off to an editor to be proofread and edited. This process can take two to four weeks depending on the workload of the editor.

Phase 5: Layout, Cover, and Hooks

Once the manuscript is edited, we'll go through and make sure all your "hooks" for marketing purposes are properly inserted. We'll also lay out the copy into a format necessary to publish the book, as well as design the cover.

Figure about one to two weeks, depending on whether we go with a custom-designed cover or standard cover. It will all depend on the audience and purpose for the book. We'll decide on this during the project.

Phase 6: Final Proofing and Proof Copy

We take another final look at everything one more time and upload the book to CreateSpace to get it approved. We will order a physical copy of the book to be sent to us for review. We'll go through that physical copy carefully and make sure the cover is right, all the pages line up, and the book looks ready for publishing.

This process takes one to three weeks, depending on the speed of Amazon and whether we need to submit any changes.

If everything is perfect, we'll finalize the project, and your book will be on Amazon.com within a week. At this point, you will be a published author. Once you catch your breath, we will discuss how to turn this book into high-paying clients and customers!

Details

The minimum length of your book should be 12,500 words to get at least a 100-page paperback book measuring 5.25" by 8".

Most books are between 125 and 175 pages, give or take 25 pages. That will be our goal. Books need to be as long as they need to be – meaning long enough to deliver the story and message completely and not any longer than that.

The type of book, the proper length of the book, and the material used for the book are all determined during the pre-interview, interview, and writing process.

It's Your Story . . .

This is all about *your* story. The most critical part of a growing business is the story, and those that can tell the most compelling story tend to have the most success.

I know there are other self-publishing options for you to choose from, and you will find several at this price range. What makes my process different from everyone else's is I am an experienced author, coach, and radio-show host, gifted at leading you in the storytelling process. I know how to create books that tell a story and sell a concept. I know how to sell *you*! Together we will create a compelling story that makes people desire more of you, and seek to engage in more of what you have to offer.

This book will be an asset to help you get more visibility, more clients, more speaking engagements, more interviews, more credibility, and more authority in your marketplace.

I can't wait to get started with you!

Final Thoughts

I hope you've enjoyed the book and have learned a few things along the way.

My goals for this book were to give you a resource to help you understand the value of a book, help you make a decision on whether writing a book is right for you and determine the best way for you to get a book done, and guide you in the option you pick.

I'd love an opportunity to speak with you and guide you on your journey to becoming an author.

I wish you much joy, peace, and success!

—Bob

If you have any questions, please see
www.MyBookDone.com

Watch the FREE webinar *Self-Publish!*
or Contact Bob Regnerus
at Bob@RJRComputing.com
or 877–349–2615

Resources

Editors

Joanne Asala, a Chicago native, is an accomplished author and editor with more than twenty years of experience in book, magazine, educational, and business publishing. Skilled in both print and online editing, Joanne holds a bachelor's degree in English from the University of Iowa and is certified in tech writing and editing. She handles the majority of the editing at Compass Rose Horizons, but if there is a particular project that she feels is better suited for another editor, she will work with you to find the right one. She is also skilled in e-book conversion and basic book design. Joanne and her fiancé currently live in Evanston, Illinois, where they are hard at work restoring a 1920s-era brick home.

Find Joanne online at www.compassrose.com

Designers

Designers come and go. If you cannot locate one on Craigslist.org or CreateSpace.com, contact my office for a current referral.

Book Marketing

There are a lot of experts in the book marketing space, let alone the thousands of PR agencies that specialize in working with authors to get interviews and sell more books. I've corresponded with dozens of people over the years. My suggestion is that if you decide on a PR agent, interview that person well and ask for references from authors in a similar market/market space as you and see how they performed.

For you do-it-yourselfers out there, I've seen a number of people helping authors, but I particularly like John Kremer. I've interviewed him on the radio, and he is the real deal.

John Kremer is the author of *1001 Ways to Market Your Books*, the developer and editor of http://BookMarket.com, and a book marketing and Internet marketing consultant.

John is an industry veteran and humble expert who helps thousand of authors use new and time-tested strategies to get books sold, get noticed in a crowd, and use a book for growing a business. John has many innovative ways to get you and your book attention that fit any budget.

Book Publishing

Printing and Distribution: Amazon's CreateSpace:

https://www.createspace.com

Printing Only: **48** Hour Books:

http://www.48hrbooks.com

Made in the USA
Charleston, SC
28 September 2013